Music Minus One Vocals

BROADWAY
Duets

mmo
2148

BROADWAY *Duets*

CONTENTS

ISBN 978-1-941566-48-0

MMO 2148

What Do The Simple Folk Do?

from "Camelot"

Words and Music by
Alan Jay Lerner and Frederick Loewe

*For duet segments, vocal parts are
shown stems up and stems down*

6

We Kiss In A Shadow
from "Camelot"

Words and Music by
Alan Jay Lerner and Frederick Loewe

*For duet segments, vocal parts are
shown stems up and stems down*

Summer Nights

from "Grease"

**Words and Music by
Warren Casey and Jim Jacobs**

*For duet segments, vocal parts are
shown stems up and stems down*

1. Sum - mer lov - in, had me a blast, Sum - mer lov - in,
2. She swam by me, she got a cramp. He ran by me,
3. Took her bowl - ing in the ar - cade, We went stroll - ing,

happ - ened so fast. Met a girl, cra - zy for me,
got my suit damp. Saved her life, she near - ly drowned!
drank le - mon - ade. We made out un - der the dock.

Met a boy, cute as can be. Sum - mer days,
He showed off, splash - ing a - round. Sum - mer sun,
We stayed out till ten o clock Sum - mer fling,

drift - ing a - way, to uh, oh those sum - mer nights. Well a, well a, well a
some - thing's be - gun, But, uh, oh those sum - mer nights. Well a well a well a
don't mean a thing But,

Uh, tell me more, tell me more, did you get ve - ry far? Tell me more, tell me
uh Tell me more, tell me more, was it love at first sight? Tell me more, tell more

more, like does he have a car?
more, Did she put up a fight?

I Remember It Well

from "Gigi"

Words and Music by
Alan Jay Lerner and Frederick Lowe

Think Of Me
from "Phantom Of The Opera"

**Words and Music by
Charles Hart, Richard Stilgoe
and Andrew Lloyd Webber**

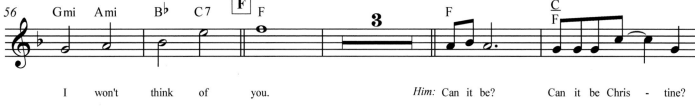

People Will Say We're In Love

from "Oklahoma!"

Words and Music by
Oscar Hammerstein II and Jerome Kern

19

MMO 2148

Bess, You Is My Woman Now

from "Porgy and Bess"

Words and Music by
DuBose and Dorothy Heyward, Ira Gershwin,
and George Gershwin

Make Believe

from "Show Boat"

Words and Music by
Oscar Hammerstein II and Jerome Kern

For duet segments, vocal parts are shown stems up and stems down

MMO 2148

It Only Takes A Moment

from "Hello, Dolly"

Words and Music by
Jerry Herman

For duet segments, vocal parts are
shown stems up and stems down

All I Ask Of You

from "Phantom Of The Opera"

Words and Music by
Charles Hart, Richard Stilgoe,
and Andrew Lloyd Webber

For duet segments, vocal parts are shown stems up and stems down

Music Minus One
50 Executive Boulevard • Elmsford, New York 10523-1325
914-592-1188 • e-mail: info@musicminusone.com
www.musicminusone.com

MMO 2148

ISBN 978-1-941566-48-0